dear Celin ♡
choosing friends is one of the [...] young people can make as fri[...] attitudes, behaviors, and overall growth.
dear Celin ps look for friends, who share your core values such as honesty, kindness, and respect.

CHOOSE GOOD FRIENDS (AND KEEP THEM)

with lot's of love Edward babie & Nassi ♡

DR. GINA ABA WOOD ESHUN

GINAWESH PUBLISHERS

Copyright © 2023 DR. GINA ABA WOOD ESHUN

All rights reserved

The characters and events portrayed in this book are fictitious. Any similarity to real persons, living or dead, is coincidental and not intended by the author.

No part of this book may be reproduced, or stored in a retrieval system, or transmitted in any form or by any means, electronic, mechanical, photocopying, recording, or otherwise, without express written permission of the publisher.

ISBN: 9798391209751

Cover design by: Art Painter
Library of Congress Control Number: 2018675309
Printed in the United States of America

CONTENTS

Title Page
Copyright
Introduction
CHAPTER 1.
YOU ARE NOT ALONE 1
CHAPTER 2. 5
WHO IS A FRIEND? 6
CHAPTER 3. 10
CHOOSING YOUR FRIENDS 11
CHAPTER 4. 14
4 TESTS FOR LASTING FRIENDSHIPS 15
CHAPTER 5. 18
HINDRANCES TO LASTING FRIENDSHIPS 19
CHAPTER 6. 25
BREAK AWAY FROM BAD FRIENDS 26
CHAPTER 7. 31
THE BUCK STOPS WITH YOU 32
Acknowledgement 35
About The Author 37
Books By This Author 39

INTRODUCTION

Choose Good Friends (And Keep Them), is just for you. Yes, you dear reader. This book deals with many of the nagging issues young people are confronted with in their daily lives as they relate to the people around them as their friends.

Some young people have gone wayward because of bad advice given by their friends (peers). Thank God some have ended up well by not following such bad advice, but rather heeded good advice by their parents and other well meaning adults.

2 Things To Do When You Need Answers To Your Questions

Dear reader, whenever you do not have the answers you need about particular issues in life. Do these two things.

1. Pray about the issue asking the Holy Spirit to lead you to examples of your situation in the Bible from which you can learn some moral lessons.
2. Pray that God leads you to spirit-filled pastors, counselors, and leaders who are better placed to answer your questions.

As a Pastor, I have worked with many young people from different backgrounds for many years and have come accross many who started well with a bright life but were not able to end well because of the influence of bad friends.

For many years, it has been my desire, passion and burden to see young people do well in life and pursue their god given callings and talents.

This was the reason why I instituted the yearly Youth Arise Conference and Talents Expo and the Schools Train which focused on harnesting talents of the youth and sharing the Gospel of Jesus, in a bid to 'catch them young' for Christ who came to save the lost, sick and the perishing from age 0 to over 100 years .

I also yearn to help young people enjoy their walk with the Lord and help them surmount many of the difficulties that are prone arise during their teenage years and in their lives as young adults through christian counseling.

In this book, I attempt to advice on how to selection good friends and keep them from a biblical perception.

CHAPTER 1.

YOU ARE NOT ALONE

Dear Reader, never think that you are alone in your struggles as a young person. God is with you. God knows you. Yes He knows you inside out and is always by your side

In Jeremiah 1:5, God says to the Prophet Jeremiah,

> *"Before I formed thee in the womb, I knew you; and before you were born, I set you apart; I appointed you a prophet to the nations."*

This shows that before Jeremiah became a living being in the womb of his mother, he existed whenere God is. And it was God who created him with a plan for his life.

Think about this. It was God who appointed him to become a prophet. This explains why we all have differnt careers and professions. God in his own wisdom chose your career or profession. Do you know your call, career or profession yet? Or are you still ignorant of who the Lord has called you to be?

Beloved, take time to know yourself. You do this by trying to look into yourself for your natural creative skills passions and talents?

Search for what drives or motivates you in life and go after it. Yes! Carefully search this out as a first step.

God Is Not Boring

God is not a boring God. He wants you to have a happy, 'fun' and contented life as a Child of God. After all, he created man (including you) in his image. His image is beautiful, perfect, happy and loving. This is just what he expects you to be.

In the book of Genesis, we are introduced to Adam, the first man God created. He was given many wonderful things in the garden for his use. Indeed God placed everything he created at his disposal. He never fails to amply provide for those he loves and those who trust in him.

Also, God decided to provide a friend and helper for him because he said that it was not good for the man to be alone. I am happy God did this, because God is not a loner. He walks hand in hand with his son Jesus Christ and the Holy Spirit in perfect harmony.

Eve, was the first woman and mother of mankind (Genesis 2:8). She was his friend and helpmate. Without Eve, Adam would have been lonely and very unhappy.

Do Not Dwell On The Pleasures Of Life

So, in God's plan, he created space for friends who are be our helpers and shoulders for us to lean on in our journey of life and when difficulties arise.

But he does not expect us to join hands with our friends to do negative things. God is displeased when we do not give him credit for the good things he gives us.

Adam and Eve tried to disregard God's love and guidedance and lost their paradise. They sought the pleasures of life (apple) and lost all they had by falling for the manipulation of the evil one (serpent) who caused them to sin before God.

Dear friend, do to take positive steps to make your friendships beneficial and shun people with negative lifestyles. If you go after bad friends who have nothing much to offer you, they will lead you into sin and away away from God.

In Luke 22:16-21 Jesus told a parable about a rich man who became so wealthy and forgot about the "Godfactor." He mistakenly thought his wealth had come through his own efforts and bragged like this;

> *"...And I will say to myself," you have plenty of good things laid up for many years. Take life easy; eat, drink, and be merry." (Luke 11:19)*

I believe that the rich man was a young man because he thought he had many more years to enjoy life. But God was unhappy with his attitude. He chose to disregard him and not acknowledge Him as the source of his wealth. He was so arroganct and ungrateful. So, God said to him;

> *"... You fool! This very night your life will be demanded from you. Then who will get what you have prepared?" (Luke 11:20)*

Indeed, God is the provider of every good blessing in our lives. Blessings are rewards God pours upon the righteous, so, we must acknowledge and thank him for his graciousness, no matter how small we think the blessing is.

Declaration

Now let's pause here for a declaration about our purpose to end well. Fill out appropraitely and read it aloud three times.

I, _____ (Name) Decree today that I am the selected of the Lord God who has the master plan of my destiny in his hands.

God has ordained me to be a _____ (Insert appropraitely as applies to you) (Doctor, prophet, teacher, pilot, pastor, footballer, fashion designer, musician, lawyer, evangelist, architect, pilot, air hostess/steward or farmer, etc.).

I declare that I will not miss my destiny, but will end up well to the glory of His holy name. Amen

CHAPTER 2.

WHO IS A FRIEND?

We all have friends. Friends are people we know who are not part of our families; they can be neighbors and acquaintances or people we recently met. We have friends from school, our neighbourhood, or from the Church we belong to, among many others.

They may be older or younger than us, or can be people above or below us on the social ladder. Friends can be people of the opposite or the same sex. Indeed man yearns for companionship and as already stated, without friends, man would be such a lonely soul.

Some Definitions

Who is a friend? Let us consider a some definitions;
Friendship generally, can be described as a mutual relationship between two individuals who respect and trust each other.

According to Aristotle, a friend is, "a single soul living in two bodies."

The Collins Shorter Dictionary and Thesaurus defines,a friend as, "one well known to another and regarded with affection and loyalty, an intimate associate or a supporter."

From the above definition, we can conclude that, we all need friends who must be affectionate and loyal to us. Like our relatives, friends can also form a support base around us when we have no family members around to look out for us. Friends can watch our backs and give us the emotional fulfillment we need.

But, just as we expect our friends to be beneficial to us, can we also be trusted to support them when they also need us for worthy causes?

Jesus used a story in Luke 11:5-8, to show that friendship is a means which allows people to ask for favors from others.

He explains;

> *Then said to them, 'Suppose one of you has a friend, and he goes to him at midnight and says, 'Friend, lend me three loaves of bread because a friend of mine on a journey has come to me and I have nothing to set before him. Then the one inside answers, "Don't bother me. The door is already locked, and my children are with me in bed. I can't get up and give you anything. I tell you, though he will not get up and give him the bread because he is his friend, yet because of the man's boldness, he will give him as much as he needs." (Luke 11:5-8)*

Beloved, the lesson from the above story is that a good friend will never let you down when you need him/her most. That is why Proverbs 18:24 says that, some friends may do for us what some of our relatives may not do.

Although having too many friends may lead to destruction (too many cooks spoil the broth), it is possible to have friends who love and care for us more than our relatives.

> *A man of many companions may come to ruin, but there is a friend who sticks closer than a brother. (Proverbs 18:24)*

David And Jonathan

One good example of such a great friendship in the Bible, is the one between Jonathan and David. 1st Samuel 20:17 states;

> *… Jonathan caused David to swear again because he loved him: for he loved him as he loved his soul. (1 Samuel 20:17)*

> *And it came to pass that when he had made an end of speaking unto Saul, that the soul of Jonathan was knit with the soul of David, and Jonathan loved him as his Soul (1 Samuel 18: 1).*

Soul Tie Relationship

Sometimes, friends may be inseparable. Oftentimes a soul-tie relationship may have been formed. So, we must be careful to choose friends who love and worship God because friendship can be a bridge for physical and spiritual knitting of souls.

If we choose evil or ungodly friends, we become yoked indirectly to the power which controls them. For this reason, we ourselves must live godly to be good role models to them. With this, so that our effort to win them over for Christ will not be so difficult.

Beloved, never hide your identity as a Christian. Stand up boldly for Christ wherever you are. Jesus loves you so much, and you have so much to gain by standing up for him and declaring that you belong to him. Everyone will know your stand and this will keep you protected from bad friends.

CHAPTER 3.

CHOOSING YOUR FRIENDS

Most people have experienced friendship with many people than one. Many of us can testify that for one reason or the other, we become close friends with particular people and not others.

Sometimes, we cannot understand the reason for the attraction, although sometimes we are attracted by the special qualities and talents among others that people have.

And in certain instances, some of our friends have become closer to us than our brothers and sisters. Proverbs 18:24 says it all:

> *"A man of many companions may come to ruin, but there is a friend who sticks closer than a brother." (Proverbs 18:24)*

Dear friend, pray about your friends before accepting them into your life. This practise means you allow God to lead you in the selection of your friends. Ceratainly God will help you to know which ones will bring you gain or pain.

The Battle

Are you aware that there is a never ending spiritual battle between good and evil? Both Jesus Christ, the Son of the living God and the devil desire to have more converts for their kingdoms, ie the kingdom of light and the kingdom of darkness respectively. Let us do our best to be in the winning camp of Jesus Christ.

It will be good to be concious of the fact that people with wrong spirits, can convert people with right spirits and vice-versa. That is why Apostle Paul advises,

> *"Do not be unequally yoked with unbelievers. For what fellowship hath righteousness with unrighteousness? And what communion hath darkness with light? (2 Corinthians 6:14)*

Paul emphasized the need to look before leaping. choose friends who are born again believers, God fearing and Christ-like in their conduct. You must break away from any ungodly friends to gain the favour of God.

> *In 2 Corinthians 6:17-18, God is clearly s*

In 2nd Corinthians 6:17-18, God clearly states,

> *"Therefore, come out from them and be separate, says the Lord. Touch no unclean thing and I will receive you. I will be a father to you, and you will be my sons and daughters, says the Lord Almighty." (2 Corinthians 6:17-18)*

What a good God and Father we serve! He promises take good care of us if we choose not to be yoked with the ungodly.

Jesus chose all his disciples with special care, and demanded that they would be self-denying and cross-bearing following after him. This should be our model to follow as we choose our friends.

CHAPTER 4.

4 TESTS FOR LASTING FRIENDSHIPS

Human beings have different attitudes and behavior which can lead to disagreements. Because of this, sometimes, it is difficult to have lasting friendships. Yet, some people have remained friends since childhood, which means that, it is possible to have lasting friendships.

There are examples of some very good friends breaking up for various reasons (although they may attend the same church or belong to the same fellowship). But, the fact that people share the same interests or religion may not necessarily help friendships to last or grow.

For friendships to grow, they must be worked at. And, the following are four tests of lasting friendships. Let's search the scriptures;

1. Love

This is an important test which should be the foundation of every friendship. Romans 12:9-19 says,

> "Love must be sincere. Hate what is evil; cling to what is good. Be devoted to one another in brotherly love. Honor one another above yourselves."

Proverbs 10:12 is clear that, "Hatred stirs up dissension, but love covers up a multitude of sins." So, "Do not seek revenge or bear grudge against one of your people, but love your neighbor as yourself.. " (Leviticus 19:18).

It is important to heed this advice always.

> "Keep on loving each other as brothers. Do not forget to entertain strangers, for by so doing some people have entertained angels without knowing it ... " (Hebrews 13:1-3).

2. Loyalty

Another test is loyalty. It is important that friends remain loyal to each other. They must be able to stand together in moments of difficulties, and celebrate the joys of and successes of others.

> "... Do not deceive one another." (Leviticus 19:11) Lying, cheating, envy and jealousy must not be encouraged in good friendships.

3. Similar Interests:

Friends can be different in many ways; but, there has to be something that brings them together. They must have similar interests, something they agree on.

Without similar interests there will be frequent disagreements. Amos 3:3 is clear about this. Its asks, "Do two walk together unless they have agreed to do so?"

When two friends agree even God is happy with them and blesses them.

> *"I tell you the truth; if two of you on earth agree on anything you ask for it shall be done for you by my father in heaven. For where two or three come together in my name, there am I with them." (Matthew 18:19)*

4. Mutual Respect:

Respect is important for any kind of friendship. Mutual respect and equal treatment will lead to a great friendship. Leviticus 19:15 sums it up with this advice;

> *Do not pervert justice; do not show partiality to the poor or favoritism to the great, but judge your neighbor fairly. (Leviticus 19:15)*

CHAPTER 5.

HINDRANCES TO LASTING FRIENDSHIPS

Many issues destroy good friendships. This chapter discusses four of them. These are selection criteria, wrong attitudes, bad communication, skills and an unforgiving attitude.

1. Selection Criteria

A question I want to ask you is this. "What criteria do you use in the selection of your friends? Do you have an idea of the kind of people you want to befriend?

It is a necessity to be clear about who you want to be your friends. You must study people well before allowing them into your space.

Know their strengths and weaknesses and decide whether friendship with them will be mutually beneficial to both of you. Also, remember to pray to God to reveal hidden secrets about their lives to you.

As a child of God, you will benefit from hanging out with people of good morals and values who will uplift you. Avoid people with a competitive or jealous spirit who will put you down.

2. Wrong Attitudes

I know people who sulk all the time for no reason; people who decide not to speak or socialize with others because of their social status; some who love to gossip and insult others for no reason, and others who turn every conversation into a quarrel.

These are wrong attitudes which give a bad impression about us and may keep people away from us. We must learn to be friendly, lively and open-minded. God has created each one of us with different emotions and character and so, we must have a big heart to accomodate every one.

Normally, it does not pay to say all we think about to others, but at least we can be honest about who we are and what we stand for.

open to joining christian fellowship groups; as well as, taking part in music, sports, and recreational activities among others, in your school, church or neighborhood youth group whenever we have time on our hands. This will give you a sense of direction in order not to fall into bad company.

To get others to be drawn to you, participate in activities open to joining christian fellowship and evangelismgroups, the choir, choreography, music, sports, among many others.

We may never get another opportunity to meet the people God brings our way each day, so we must be bold to talk about God whenever we get the chance.

3. Bad Communication Skills

Some people have the habit of speaking all the time, not listening to what others have to say. This is not a good practice. No man is an island. We need to be good listeners, speak well, and learn to subject what we hear to good judgment

A. Good Listeners

If we learn to become good listeners, we may decode some hidden information that may be of use to us and save us from falling into pits.

Watchman Nee wrote,

> *"A servant of the lord must acquire the habit of listening to what people say. Not listening casually, but with attention. This is not easy. Our ears must be trained to hear…. bad listeners will never be good workers. Some think the main essential is to be able to speak. No, it is to be able to listen."*

B. Speak Well

In Colossians 4:6, Apostle Paul advises,

> *"Let your speech be always with grace, seasoned with salt, that ye may know how to answer every man."*

When uncertain about what to say, subject it to the word of God, or ask matured or spirit-filled Christians about it before speaking it.

In our conversations with others, we must use simple open-ended questions that will give the other person an opportunity to say, "Yes" or "No." This is a good way for most conversations to begin.

Always keep a positive attitude. Paul further commands us,

> *"to speak evil of no man, not to be brawlers, but gentle, showing all meekness unto all men. (Titus 3:2)*

Also,

> *"Do not let unwholesome talk come out of your mouths but what helps build others up according to their needs, that it may benefit those who listen." (Ephesians 4:29)*

C. Be Yourself

Child of God, be your self. Avoid pretence and do not be in the habit of "posing" or "flexing" unnecessarily. People can see through this. Instead, rely on the Holy Spirit for grace to be help you be the champion that you are.

D. A Forgiving Attitude

People are imperfect and can offend each other leading to hurt and disappointments. The imperfect nature of man was first established in the Garden of Eden by Adam and Eve. They went against God's commandment not to eat of the tree of knowledge of good and evil (Genesis 2:17). And after breaking God's law, they tried to hide from Him.

Later, God punished them, but his forgiving nature was so evident. He sewed a dress of leaves to cover their nakedness

(Genesis 3:21). May we follow God's ways by learning to forgive others whenever the need arises! Unforgiveness is a sin. It has led to the downfall of many people. Again, there is scientific proof that the root of certain illnesses such as High Blood Pressure and diabetes can be traced to an unforgiving attitude.

Because we believers have the nature of Christ in us, it should be easy for us to forgive others when they hurt us.

> *"Be kind and compassionate towards each other, forgiving each other, just as in Christ God forgave you." (Ephesians 4:32)*

A Short Exercise For You

Let us pause once again for this short exercise.
Take a sheet of paper. Write down everything that you think is a blessing from God in your life. How many blessings were you able to write down? I bet they are uncountable.

Proverbs 10:6 says, "Blessings crown the head of the righteous…" As young people, one gift that is really needed by most is wisdom. According to the Macmillan English Dictionary for Advanced Learners (International Students Edition, 2006),

> *Wisdom is the ability to make good decisions based on knowledge and experience.*

This ability is not so common because it is a gift from God. So it is needful to seek wisdom from God daily in prayer. The ability to make good decisions is not an automatic virtue. It will come to us when we go on our knees and pray to God for it.

Wise King Solomon noted;

> *"Do not forsake wisdom, and she will protect you; love her, and she will watch over you. Wisdom is supreme; therefore, get wisdom. Though it costs all you have, get an understanding. Esteem her and she will exalt you; embrace her, and she will honor you. She will set a garland of grace upon your head and present you with a crown of splendor." (Proverbs 7:6-9)*

I hope you will never forget this advice.

CHAPTER 6.

BREAK AWAY FROM BAD FRIENDS

Dear friend, this chapter contains advice to you to break away from bad friends if you have any in your life right now as they can get you into trouble and take you away from achieving your God given destiny.

It is important to make a conscious effort to break away from bad friends. But before we do, we must have a word with them about forsaking their bad ways and allow Jesus Christ to sherperd them as their Lord and personal Savior.

As a Child of God, you were filled with the Holy Spirit when you repented and believed in the salvation of Jesus Christ.

As you allow the Holy Spirit more room for control in your life, the fruit of the spirit is produced. The fruit of the spirit are love, joy, peace, patience, kindness, goodness, faithfulness, gentleness and self control (Galatians 5:22).

Operating the gifts of the spirit does not mean you must trust eeveryone. In Psalm 135:11-15, David said he mistakenly trusted some people as his friends; but they bore false witness against him, although he had given them his best.

He said,

> *"Ruthless witnesses come forward; they question me on things I know nothing about. They repay me evil for good and leave my soul forlorn. Yet when they were ill, I put on sackcloth and humbled myself with fasting. When my prayers returned to me unanswered, I went about mourning as though for my friend or brother. I bowed my head in grief as though weeping for my mother, but when I stumbled, they gathered in glee; attackers gathered against me when I was unaware. They slandered me without ceasing. Like the ungodly they maliciously mocked, they gnashed their teeth at me." (Psalm 135:11-15)*

Yes, sometimes your friends may become your enemies for nothing you have done

Do Not Be A Hypocrite

It is obvious from David's narration, he had friends who pretended to be his friend when they thought evil about him. Hypocricy is so common.

There have been stories of people who pretended to be friends with others when they did not like or respect them. Many friends fall out each day because of broken trust and betrayal.

May we not be found to be hypocrites or people who cannot be trusted.

May we like David, have good thoughts about our friends, help them in any way we can, and pray for them.

Jesus said to his disciples,

> "If anyone would come after me, he must deny himself and take up his cross and follow me. (Matthew 16:21)

Like Jesus, we must decide on what we expect from our friends. Oftentimes, we meet new people we know nothing about who we allow into our circle of friends.

Meet God's Standards

It would be good to have proper background checks, and carefully watch out to see if our new and old acquaintances meet God's standards. If they do not, you have no business with them except trying to soul win them.

The Great Commision

It is our responsibility to win over everyone who does not know Christ. Daniel 12:3 says,

> "Those who are wise will shine like the brightness of heavens, and those who lead many to righteousness, like the stars for ever and ever."

Yes! God is trusting us to go out there to win souls for him. No one is to be left out in the campaign for Jesus Christ.

As we respond to the Commission of winning souls we are seen by God as wise. Proverbs 11:30 says, "…and he who wins souls is wise."

Furthermore, soul winners have a reward which will last forever. "Those who lead many to righteousness, as the stars will shine forever and ever." (Daniel 12:3). Beloved get ready to shine in every endevor.

Hell is real andmany souls are bound for hell fire. We can to depopulate Hell by telling them the good news about Jesus Christ and how he came to die so that man's sins might be forgiven and their souls be received into God's eternal glory.

Jesus said;

> *"All authority in heaven and on earth has been given to me. Therefore, go and make disciples of all nations baptizing them in the name of the Father, Son, and the Holy Spirit and teaching them to obey everything I have commanded you. And surely, I am with you always to the end of the age" (Matthew 28:19-20).*

This is the Great Commission.

The Parable Of The Banquet

Again, The Great Commission is further explained by our Lord in the Parable of the Banquet (Matthew 22:1-10). The story is about a king who made a marriage banquet for his son and invited many guests who refused to attend for their various personal reasons.

So, the king said to his servants;

> *"The wedding is ready, but those I invited did not deserve to come. Go to the street corners and invite to the*

> *banquet anyone you find" So the servants went out into the streets and gathered all the people they could find, both good and bad, and the wedding hall was filled with guests." (Matthew 22:8-10)*

God has made salvation available to all. May you be able to invite all your friends and anyone around you to partake in this grace.

CHAPTER 7.

THE BUCK STOPS WITH YOU

I have had the occasion to hear people accusing others for gossiping about them; being involved in backbiting or spreading falsehoods; or doing other acts to show what bad friend they are.

In Paul's letter to the Ephesians he admonishes;

> *"Therefore, each of you must put off falsehood and speak truthfully to his neighbor, for we are all the members of one body." (Ephesians 4:25)*

Although gossiping comes naturally to some people, we must make a conscious effort not to gossip about others. Proverbs 16:13 states;

> *"Kings take pleasure in honest lips; they value a man who speaks the truth. (Proverbs 16:3)*

Also, we must learn to be truthful, not spread rumors or tell tales about others.

Proverbs 18:6-8 states,

> *"A fool's lips bring him strife, and his mouth invites a beating. A fool's mouth is his undoing and his lips a snare to his soul. The words of a gossip are like choice morsels they go down to a man's innermost parts."*

Proverbs 18: 19-21 add;

> *"An offended brother is more yielding than a fortified city, and disputes are like the barred gates of a citadel. From the fruit of his mouth, a man's stomach is filled; with the harvest from his lips, he is satisfied. The tongue has the power of life and death and those who love it will eat its fruit."*

Whatever we use our lips for, we get in return. If we use it to teach or praise, we receive the same and vice versa. The tongue is a small member of the body which can cause a lot of havock if not tamed. James Chapter 3 teaches about the importance of taming the tongue.

Dear Friend, uphold the virtue of honesty and integrity. Let people know that you are a person of both virtues.

Choosing good friends is not an easy job. If you follow the advice given in this book, you will be able to carefully choose them and keep them . Do you get me?

DR. GEORGINA ABA WOOD ESHUN

ACKNOWLEDGEMENT

I acknowledge all the Foundation members of Christian International Youth Club (2009) who gave meaning and understanding to my God given passion, mission and vision for the youth.

ABOUT THE AUTHOR

Rev. Dr. Gina Aba Wood Eshun

Rev. Dr. Gina Aba Wood Eshun is a Journalist, Author and an International Empowerment Speaker. Georgina holds a PhD in Christian Philosophy (Theology) from Christian Leadership University, U.S.A. She is married to George Eshun and they have a son Kweku Ofori Eshun (Kuuku).

BOOKS BY THIS AUTHOR

Self Deliverance Tactics To Break Evil Soul Ties

So you were involved in a relationship (sexual, family or spiritual etc.) and cannot understand why you can't seem to forget about your former partner/family relations/group even though you are not with them any more. This has made it difficult for you to move on and you cannot figure out why. Issues about the probability of a soul tie being formed keep coming up and you just need some answers.This book discusses all about soul ties and gives some tactics on how you can break away from negative soul ties through self deliverance prayers. Are you ready for the prayer battle?

Ebook Publishing For Wealth On Amazon

This Book will teach you how to self-publish on Amazon for wealth. It takes you through various processes in writing your book, publishing it, and the various financial processes to receIve your funds from Amazon. It also teaches how you can consult for others by publishing their books.

Printed in Great Britain
by Amazon